THE
INCREDIBLE
HERE
AND NOW

THE PLAY

Felicity Castagna

RIVERSIDE | NATIONAL THEATRE
ᴼ PARRAMATTA
ꜰ

Currency Press,
Sydney

CURRENT THEATRE SERIES

First published in 2017
by Currency Press Pty Ltd,
PO Box 2287, Strawberry Hills, NSW, 2012, Australia
enquiries@currency.com.au
www.currency.com.au

in association with National Theatre of Parramatta

Copyright: *The Incredible Here and Now: The Play* © Felicity Castagna, 2017.

Adapted from novel, first published by Giramondo Publishing Company, 2013.
www.giramondopublishing.com

Cataloguing-in-publication data for this title is available from the National
Library of Australia website: www.nla.gov.au

Typeset by Dean Nottle for Currency Press.
Cover and program design by Tristan Ceddia.
Cover photography by Joanne Kee.

Currency Press acknowledges the Traditional Owners of the Country on which
we live and work. We pay our respects to all Aboriginal and Torres Strait
Islander Elders, past and present.

Contents

The Incredible Here and Now was first produced by National Theatre of Parramatta at Riverside Theatres, Parramatta, on 13 July 2017, with the following cast:

MONIQUE / KATE / JOE	Libby Asciak
MUM	Caroline Brazier
DOM	Alex Cubis
MICHAEL	Bardiya McKinnon
SHADI	Ryan Peters
POPPY / PRINCIPAL / MONIQUE'S DAD	Sal Sharah
LEENA / ESTHER / SAL	Olivia Simone

Directors, Jeneffa Soldatic and Wayne Harrison
Set and Costume Designer, Isabel Hudson
Sound Designer, Séan Van Doornum
Lighting Designer, Martin Kinanne
Movement Director, Sara Black
Production Manager, Damion Holling
Stage Manager, Kirsty Walker
Creative Futures Participant, Concey Bosco
Drone Videographer, Tristan Baker

CHARACTERS

MICHAEL
DOM
SHADI
MUM
POPPY
PRINCIPAL
MONIQUE'S DAD
LEENA
SAL
ESTHER
MONIQUE
KATE
JOE

The following characters may be played by actors, or by voice-over:

TEACHER
SCHOOLBOYS
ESTHER'S SON
JOURNALIST
POLICE RIOT SQUAD OFFICER
LEBANESE MAN
INDIAN WOMAN
SECURITY GUARD

Suggested doubling:

POPPY / PRINCIPAL / MONIQUE'S DAD
LEENA / ESTHER / SAL
MONIQUE / KATE / JOE

SETTING

The action of the play takes place in the middle of the theatre with the audience on two sides of the performance. On one side of the stage there is a car and on the other a scaffolding tower with a diving board on top. There are three large screens for projection on the walls.

This play went to press before the end of rehearsals and may differ from the play as performed.

ACT ONE

SCENE ONE

The PRINCIPAL *ushers the audience from the lobby into the theatre. His following lines are also pre-recorded: these recordings are projected onto the screens inside the theatre, playing the same lines that he is saying in real-time in the lobby.*

Inside the theatre we are at a boys' school in Parramatta. The sound of an engine revving marks the beginning of the play. MICHAEL *and* SHADI *lean against the car.*

PRINCIPAL: Now you!

> JOE *runs through the lobby and circles around some of the audience as the* PRINCIPAL *points at him, before he runs off into the theatre.*

This is not a race. I said walk don't run. Exit the school in an orderly fashion. The summer holidays will still be there in another five minutes. You'll have all the time in the world, shortly, to grow as men, to contemplate your futures, to become wiser, older more sure of yourself … or to walk around and around and around Parramatta Westfield like you're stuck inside a goldfish bowl, and breakdance in the parking lot of McDonald's and get idiotic haircuts and install illegal blue lights under your busted-up cars and embarrass yourself with the ladies in the Eastern suburbs. No-one's listening to me are you? You're all a bunch of ridiculous-looking monkeys walking around like your body parts don't fit together, sagging your pants so low your butt cracks stick out, acting like what you've got between your legs is so large you've got to walk bowlegged. Walk don't run. Life's not a race. No need to get anywhere so quickly. Walk. You're going to run each other over. Exit the school in an orderly fashion. You've got so many more summers ahead of you. Walk. Don't run. Be safe.

> DOM *makes a dramatic entrance and ends up standing on top of the car.*

MICHAEL: [*to the audience*] There's my older brother Dom now, making his usual entrance, like the biggest guy in school that he is. But I'm sure you all know him anyway. Ladies' man. Best car in the West. He's like Dominic Toretto from *The Fast and The Furious* movies, walking around the place with his crew like he just can't help but grab everyone's attention.

DOM *gives an acknowledging gesture to* MICHAEL.

And that's my best mate Shadi.

DOM *nods his head at* SHADI. *They all admire the car, running their hands across it, flexing their muscles in front of it, checking out what they look like in the mirrors. We hear the revving of an engine again. The revving competes with the sounds of the schoolyard.* JOE *crawls cautiously out of the boot of the car with a red flag and walks towards the centre of the stage. He waves the flag dramatically in front of the* PRINCIPAL *to begin the race out of the schoolyard. There is the sound of tyres screeching.*

MICHAEL: It's the last day of school before holidays. None of them boys can make it out those gates fast enough.

DOM: And they're off!

DOM *grabs* MICHAEL *and hauls him up to stand on the car boot/ bonnet.* SHADI *stands next to the car getting ready to run.*

PRINCIPAL: Walk. Don't run. Be sensible. Exit the school in an orderly fashion.

DOM: And oh! The Asians are gaining on the Islanders, they're distracted playing drums on garbage lids someone found on the ground and here come the Serbs. They're moving in from the outside lanes and no! They faltered on the turn past the demountables. The Everything Elses are gaining ground now, they're moving in, they're way out ahead, but no! No! Unbelievable. Last minute the Lebs move into the lead.

SHADI *looks excited as if his car is about to win the race.*

They've changed lanes and cut every other guy off. Almost. They're ahead by a nose, but no! They're in the lead. The Lebs are in first position.

SHADI: That's my crew!

SHADI *puts his arms up like he is the race champion.* MICHAEL *shakes* SHADI'*s hand in a gesture of congratulations and* SHADI *runs off the stage.*

DOM: They've won! And the Lebs have taken it. First over the line. Last day of school.

JOE *walks slowly and cautiously out onto the stage again. He looks like he lacks confidence at first, but then he straightens himself up and starts to walk confidently in a 'manly' fashion across the stage. All the available actors run across the stage, knock him over from behind and keep running.*

MICHAEL: [*adopting the same body language and tone as* DOM] But it's not over yet, folks! No! We've got one boy down. It's that pimple-faced kid, Joe, everyone loves to run over—

DOM: The one who was on the front page of the *Daily Telegraph*, the one who told all those reporters that in the West it's easier to get a gun than a pizza—

JOE: Never seen a gun—

MICHAEL: Like the rest of us, but he sure as hell knows how to eat a pizza. And he's down—

DOM: He's out—

PRINCIPAL: Walk. Don't run. Be sensible.

He looks at JOE *who is moaning on the ground. He grabs his arms and drags him offstage.* MICHAEL *and* DOM *climb off the car and strike relaxed poses, leaning against the car.* DOM *slides his hands into his pockets in a signature move that he will repeat throughout the play.*

MICHAEL *directly addresses the audience.* DOM *slowly walks around the car admiring it.*

MICHAEL: [*to the audience*] And now. Summertime. When me and Dom work really hard at keeping busy while Mum and Poppy are off working at the family electrical shop all day and Aunty Leena's off doing ... Aunty Leena things.

DOM: This is *the* shit.

MICHAEL: We go raging crazy when there's nothing doing; crazy the way we steal Best of Bollywood videos from those spice and DVD shops crammed into the front of old houses in Harris Park. We spend hours at the park poking around the old convict gravestones where the beer bottles stick out of the grass like some kind of deranged plant.

DOM: A 2001 Ford Falcon XR6, blue with a thin white stripe all the way down both sides of the body.

MICHAEL: Iridescent paint. Illegal blue lights under the tray.

DOM: Nothin' but Ford.

MICHAEL: Worth ten times more than all those Saturdays and Sundays you had to work at McDonald's to buy it.

> KATE *enters the stage. She is carrying a Coke can casually in her hand.* DOM *leans against the car, looking cool as soon as he sees her.* MICHAEL *imitates the same pose.*

You together?

DOM: Yeah … This week anyways.

KATE: What you doin'?

> KATE *sips her Coke.*

DOM: Nothin'.

> *He takes the Coke from* KATE *and has a sip.*

MICHAEL: Nothin'.

DOM: Just hanging.

> KATE *attempts to take the can of Coke back. There is a playful exchange, then* DOM *runs it down her arm.*

MICHAEL: [*watching* KATE *and* DOM *intently*] Yeah.

> KATE *leans against the car next to* DOM. *They all do different 'cool' poses against the car, taking selfies and other shots with their phones. They act like they are checking out everyone who walks past.* MICHAEL *imitates everything that* DOM *does until* KATE *leans against* DOM *and* DOM *starts to stroke her hair.*

DOM: I could eat your hair.

> *She looks at him like she is thinking of sex and* MICHAEL *stares at them before getting embarrassed and looking away.* DOM *looks at* MICHAEL *and gives him an 'I can't help being so desirable' shrug.* KATE *drags* DOM *away and* MICHAEL *looks at them shyly but with clear admiration.*

SCENE TWO

It is evening. DOM *is driving home from a party. He wears a baseball cap.* MICHAEL *is in the front passenger seat.* SHADI *is in the back seat with a couple of* BOYS. *They are carrying on like they've had a great night.* MICHAEL *and* DOM *are much more quiet. They both seem like they're off in their own world that is separate from the others.*

SHADI: Eastern Suburbs girls, bro.

BOY 1: Got to get out there to those parties more often.

BOY 2: Heaps more blondes. And more, like, ponytails and less like loud, loud colours.

SHADI: Yeah, bro, like heaps more exotic and shit than out West.

> *Without looking behind,* DOM *reaches back and whacks* SHADI *in the head.*

Ay! What was that for?

DOM: Sick of hearing about Eastern Suburbs girls.

MICHAEL: [*to* DOM] Don't be like that. That chick, Jane. She just didn't realise who you are and all that. Didn't realise you're like *the* Dom, the Dominic Toretto Dom, and like the girls out West can't get enough of you.

> DOM *doesn't respond. There is silence from everyone in the car for a while. There are flashes across the screen and/or stage that look like the red-and-white lights of cars passing by.*

The night is full-up with the red tail-lights of cars and the rims of hub caps.

> DOM *lets out an exasperated sigh and leans further back into his chair.*

DOM: Why you gotta talk like that?

MICHAEL: Like what?

DOM: Like you're Shakespeare or some shit. The night is full-up with the red tail-lights of cars and crap.

MICHAEL: You've just got your feelings all messed up because you broke up with Kate again.

> DOM *stops the car.*

DOM: Alright. Everyone out.

The BOYS *and* SHADI *walk off in different directions.* DOM *parks the car and* MICHAEL *and* DOM *get out of the car. They sit themselves down at a table. Now they are in a charcoal chicken shop. There is an image of chickens turning around on a stick on the screens. Someone brings them charcoal chicken with Lebanese bread and accompanying condiments.* DOM *rolls sandwiches like a pro.* MICHAEL *gets the ingredients all over himself. There are laughs and quiet affectionate gestures between them.*

MICHAEL: This is what night-time is made for.

DOM: Charcoal chicken.

MICHAEL *spills something down his front.*

Never gonna get a girl like that, bro.

MICHAEL: Maybe. One day—

DOM: I'll teach you everything I know one day.

MICHAEL: I'm already writing it all down.

DOM: Yeah. I know. You would.

There is the flash of red tail-lights across a screen. DOM *looks into the distance, smiles and speaks in a serious tone.*

The night is full-up with the red tail-lights of cars and the rims of hub caps.

DOM *gets out his phone, removes his cap and takes a selfie of himself and* MICHAEL.

MICHAEL: What'd you do to your hair?

DOM: Got zigzags shaved into the sides.

MICHAEL: You look like a dickhead.

DOM: It was eight bucks.

MICHAEL: Eight bucks? Ripped off. I would have done it with Mum's lady razor for two.

DOM: You're just jealous I'm so gorgeous.

MICHAEL: Mum's gonna kill you.

DOM *stands up excitedly and his face is lit up by a set of white car lights that are brighter than the lights in the previous scene.*

DOM: Look! There it is. It's that Pontiac Trans Am.

MICHAEL *stands and is lit up by the same lights.*

MICHAEL: The night is full up with the taillights of cars and dickheads with eight-dollar haircuts.

DOM: Mum's not gonna kill me. Nothing bad could ever happen here.

The scene ends with both of their faces filled with light.

SCENE THREE

Morning in Michael and Dom's apartment. Images of apartment blocks on the back screens. MUM *is in her dressing-gown.* POPPY, LEENA *and* MICHAEL *are dressed. They are drinking coffee, reading newspapers, hanging.* MICHAEL *grins and nods his head like he knows something amazing is about to happen which none of the others are privy to.*

KATE *is standing on a different part of the stage that is separate from the main action. She looks angry.* DOM *walks up to her, looking dishevelled.* KATE *pushes him playfully away and* DOM *keeps coming back to her until she gives him one last push and he is propelled toward the main action of the play with a carton of eggs underneath his arm.*

MICHAEL: [*to the audience*] Sunday morning, our place. Watch. Watch this. Everyone's been up for hours. Aunty Leena picked Poppy up from the retirement home ages ago so they could both come over for their regular Sunday morning visit. Dom's still not home.

LEENA: [*to* DOM] I brought Poppy over an hour ago.

DOM: Aunty Leena! Poppy! Nice to see you.

He greets them.

I got the eggs! I just popped out, you know, before Mum got up so I could make us all some pancakes for breakfast.

LEENA: So what time is your curfew again?

DOM: Had to go to a couple of shops.

LEENA: You smell like cigarettes.

DOM: Mum loves her pancakes on Sunday mornings—

LEENA *smells* DOM.

LEENA: And sex.

MUM: Best pancakes in the West.

MICHAEL: Dom doesn't even know how to boil an egg, but these mornings he makes the best pancakes you've ever had. My brother the genius.

DOM: Had to get the eggs ... for my gorgeous mother.

MICHAEL: Amazing what Dom gets away with. Everyone in this place got so many excuses. Like when Aunty Leena got caught pole dancing at Collectors and she said—

LEENA: You can take the girl out of Collectors but you can't take Collectors out of the girl.

MICHAEL: And that time that Poppy lost all that money at the races—

POPPY: Could have won it back if your mum had given me more cash.

MICHAEL: But Dom? He just looks at her. He doesn't even offer her any excuse.

DOM *is standing there whisking eggs.*

MUM: [*looking at* DOM] Look at those blue eyes. You have the most bluest, bluest eyes I've ever seen.

DOM *makes a display of taking the packet of eggs out from underneath his arm. He cracks an egg into a pan and begins to make pancakes.* MICHAEL *hands him things to cook with.* POPPY *walks around with the race pages, circling things.*

DOM: Hey Pops. I've got a tip for you. Heard it walking past the TAB this morning.

MICHAEL *and* DOM *grin at each other.*

POPPY: [looking genuinely interested] Yeah?

DOM: Buff—

MICHAEL: Oh yeah the guy upstairs was talking about that one too last week? The one who knows his trainer? Buff—

DOM: Buff ...

MICHAEL: Yeah. That's right. Buff ... Buff Naked.

POPPY *tries to find Buff Naked on the form guide.*

POPPY: Buff ... Buff ...

LEENA: What about Glue?

She whacks DOM, *who doesn't seem to get it until* MICHAEL *whispers something in his ear.*

DOM: Oh right. That's disgusting.

DOM'S *look of disgust quickly turns to one of approval and he holds his hand up for* LEENA.

High Five!

MICHAEL: Or Jizzon.

DOM: Oh yeah everyone at the RSL last week was talking about Jizzon…You know—

MICHAEL: Jizzon—

DOM: My face.

> POPPY *looks at the form guide with interest for a minute and then realises what they're doing and is mock angry.*

POPPY: Alright that's it you two. Shame on you taking advantage of an old man. After all those times I've taken you to the races and bought you endless hot chips—

DOM: And forgot to take us home—

POPPY: That was only once.

MICHAEL: Twice.

POPPY: I'll give you a tip. Don't touch your nose and your bum at the same time.

LEENA: [*to* POPPY] High five!

> MUM *looks exasperated. She puts her arm around* MICHAEL *and pulls him away from the others.*

MUM: So … tell me a story.

LEENA: I think your other son already gave you one. You know—the one about the eggs.

MUM: [*ignoring* LEENA] Michael's good at telling stories. Always watching things, always writing things down when no-one's looking. He got the top marks in English, you know.

MICHAEL: Shoosh … Mum, don't tell everyone that.

DOM: It's a boys' school. Gotta pretend you're a dick with no brains.

MICHAEL: I'll tell you a story. Dom tells everyone you named him after Dominic Toretto from *The Fast and The Furious* movies even though he was born like seven years before the first movie came out and even though you're always saying—

> *Clips from* The Fast and the Furious *begin to play on the screens. Everyone looks up at the screens.*

MUM: Aren't you interested in anything else?

DOM: But the boys think it is pretty cool of you, Mum.

LEENA: It's like the same movie every time. All, like, one hundred of them in that series.

DOM: Yeah, but sometimes the hot chicks and the buff guys are in America and sometimes they're in Brazil or Tokyo or some kind of island no-one has ever heard of.

MICHAEL: But wherever they are they've got nitrous oxide containers—

DOM: Strapped to their car boots like torpedoes shoved up their arses.

There is the sound of a car engine revving.

POPPY: Dom, Dom. It's your car. It's you. That Pontiac Trans Am.

The whole family runs towards the balcony to watch it drive down the street. A Pontiac Trans Am glides across the screen or is represented by two headlights or some other consistent symbol that will appear throughout the play.

DOM: It's a sign.

MUM: Of what?

DOM: Of everything. It's like wherever I am. There it is and I know that everything's gonna be all good. You know?

MUM: You boys and your cars.

DOM: I'm gonna have one just like that one day. I'm a take you all out down Church Street. We'll go cruising. Late afternoons, we'll be part of the parade—

MICHAEL: You know, watching all the boys with their undercuts walking slow-motion down the street and the bikies all pulling up on the pavements 'cause they can, and the hijab mums in their Klugers—

DOM: We'll be a part of all that, you, me, Michael, Poppy, Aunty Leena.

MUM: Well I'm not listening to all that thump thump thump stuff on your stereo. I get to pick the music.

LEENA: Think I'd rather take the bus.

DOM: I live my life a quarter mile at a time. For those ten seconds or less I am free.

There is a pause before we hear the voice-over of a MAN yelling from below their apartment.

MAN: [*voice-over*] Mum, I need money. I need money. I need money fast. Mum. Do you hear me? Money. Fast.

MUM: They're at it again.

ESTHER's voice comes from above their apartment.

ESTHER: [*voice-over*] Please go away.

MICHAEL: That's Esther. Esther with her half-baked chocolate chip biscuits and teacups full of Bundy and Coke that she's always spilling down her blouse.

MAN: [*voice-over*] Mum. I need it now. Money.

ESTHER: [*voice-over*] Please. God. Please. Go.

MICHAEL: We've all been watching Esther so long, we could all tell her story. [*To* DOM] If I was going to write it I'd call it 'Loneliness'.

DOM: She's not always so quiet, but.

MICHAEL: Nah, like that time you dyed your hair all those colours and slicked it up in a multicoloured mohawk. And she said—

DOM: [*imitating* ESTHER's *voice*] Everyone will think your mother dropped acid and had sex with a peacock.

Everyone laughs.

MICHAEL: [*shouting over the balcony*] Esther, you alright?!

ESTHER: Yeah. It'll be right. It'll be okay.

MICHAEL *stands up on the car so that he is elevated above his family and takes a piece of paper out of his pocket. Vignettes from the book fill the screens and scroll across them.*

MICHAEL: Parramatta is an everywhere people kind of place. People always coming and going. There's the Indian kids down the road who think they invented cricket and the Pakistani kids next door to them who are always trying to tell them they're wrong. Some people, they come all the way from the city and some all the way from Penrith. And then there's our upstairs neighbour Esther who never goes anywhere much. My family, they're from somewhere else a long time ago, but a lot of them have been West since the convicts landed in Parramatta Cove. Poppy says—

POPPY: Those Raffertys in the street behind you are too loud because they're part Irish and part Italian and part Lebanese and that's about as loud as people can get.

MICHAEL: Mum says, when people ask you where you're from you should say—

MUM: Here, because here is where you're at.

MICHAEL: This is my mum who says all people from all places are good people except, maybe—

The sound of Hare Krishna chanting starts up across the road.

MUM: Those Hare Krishnas across the road, always keeping me awake with all that wailing.

MICHAEL: But I like it because it makes me feel like I'm going to some far-off place as I fall into sleep like I'm West but I'm everywhere all at the same time.

MICHAEL climbs off the car and walks towards the front of the stage so he can directly address the audience.

MUM gets up closer to DOM and inspects something sticking out from the side of his cap before she takes it off his head.

MUM: What's this?

DOM: Zig-zags.

He looks proud and runs his hands through it.

MUM: [*angry*] I could kill you sometimes.

DOM: You know it looks good.

MUM smiles knowingly.

MUM: You're wearing the same clothes two days in a row and you want to tell me what's fashionable?

MICHAEL: I never thought anything bad could happen here—

SCENE FOUR

Everyone has finished their pancakes and is relaxing on a Sunday afternoon. POPPY has fallen asleep with the horseracing pages. LEENA and MUM are cleaning up and DOM and MICHAEL are watching a section from one of The Fast and the Furious *movies in which there is a car race. They watch it in agony and suspense as if they don't know that the inevitable crash/explosion is about to occur. When it happens a few seconds later they are ecstatic/forlorn.*

MICHAEL & DOM: [*talking simultaneously and over each other*] Can't believe it. Did you see that? It was like the car rolled and rolled and rolled. And then, and then, they were spinning and then and then. The crash and then like Vin Diesel gets out of the car and he's like, I'm the man. I'm the man and my chest muscles are bigger than my head and like I'm walking away from this shit.

MICHAEL and DOM *imitate the body postures and stances of Brian and Dom's characters from the film while* MUM *watches them amused/exasperated and* LEENA *pokes* POPPY *and he rolls over and grunts, trying to get back to his nap.* DOM *whacks* MICHAEL *to attention.*

DOM: Alright. You be Brian and I'll be Dominic Toretto.

They 'take the stage'. There is a mock seriousness to their performance. LEENA *and* MUM *become their audience. They clear their throats and practise their poses before beginning.*

MICHAEL: [*as Brian*] The day I got my license I got my first speeding ticket. Behind the wheel everything else just disappeared. No past, no future, no problems … just the moment.

DOM: [*as Dom*] Nothing matters except the people in this room. They are the here and now.

MUM *and* LEENA *clap.*

LEENA: Alright. I'm calling it for the morning. Let's get out.

She tries to rouse POPPY. *He rolls over.*

POPPY: [*still asleep*] Five dollars on number four.

LEENA: Well, he's no good. Need to find a gentleman to take me for a walk down the river.

She looks back and forth between DOM, MICHAEL *and* POPPY. DOM *puts himself forward and she laughs at him.*

There's nothing gentlemanly about you, buddy. [*To* MICHAEL] You'll do.

She grabs MICHAEL. DOM *offers* MUM *his arm as they exit the door and she takes it. When they exit the apartment building there is* ESTHER'S SON *looking up like he's looking for Esther. He calls out half-heartedly and doesn't seem to notice anyone.*

ESTHER'S SON: Mum. Mum.

MUM *stops smiling when she sees* ESTHER'S SON *and looks at him sadly.*

MUM: Again.

She looks up towards Esther's apartment.

Poor woman.

MICHAEL *stops and stares.* LEENA *follows his lead and stops as well.*

LEENA: There he is. Esther's son.

MICHAEL: And Esther's there alone, behind that wall and the whole world's going on outside without her.

LEENA *pulls him away. They begin to walk with* MUM *and* DOM.

LEENA: You're a good man, Michael. Wish I could find a good man like you.

MUM: Maybe if you stop hanging out at Collectors.

LEENA: Maybe you should get out there with me sometime.

MUM: And be your wing woman while you cradle snatch?

DOM: Aw burn!

MUM: Don't talk to your aunty like that.

LEENA: Everyone needs to have some fun sometimes.

DOM: Yep. Everyone needs to have some fun.

MUM: You [*referring to* DOM] need far too much fun and so does your aunt and me, I've got everything I need right here.

She takes each of her sons by the arm and walks between them. LEENA *looks left out and they leave her there that way, momentarily, before* DOM *grabs her and links arms, drawing her back in with the others.*

DOM: Look, Mum. There it is.

They go over and run their hands across/look at a bench.

MICHAEL: All those years ago. You carved your name here. So no matter how your life turned out—

MUM: I'd always know where I came from.

DOM: And you'd always know how to get back here.

SCENE FIVE

KATE, DOM *and* MICHAEL *yell out phrases back and forth and simultaneously. A bottle of hard liquor is passed back and forth.* DOM *plays with* KATE's *hair. They all take sips.* KATE *and* DOM *fondle each other and*

laugh. MICHAEL *looks on in awe and excitement. The scene is surreal.*
The music has a very different tone from that which is heard in other
parts of the play.

DOM: Oh yeah! Saturday night!
MICHAEL: Time for ice skating!
DOM: Time for a drink.
KATE: Pass the bottle.
MICHAEL: Pirouette!
KATE: Faster!
MICHAEL: Figure eights!

> DOM *is fondling* KATE *with one hand, with the other hand on*
> *the wheel. He is increasingly more interested in* KATE *than in*
> *driving.* MICHAEL *is staring at them with great admiration. They*
> *crash.* MICHAEL *goes through the windscreen.* DOM *holds out his*
> *hand to catch him but can't.*
>
> *There is a light and sound change to indicate a shift in the mood.*
> MICHAEL *stands up again slowly and looks at* DOM, *who is still in*
> *the car looking at him.* KATE *stares off into the distance and does*
> *not acknowledge either of them.*

DOM: And that's how we do it.
MICHAEL: We called it ice-skating. Ice-skating but with cars. And you
    were like—
DOM: And I was like Vin Diesel. Huge. Biggest guy in the car—
MICHAEL: Like we had nitrous oxide containers—
DOM: Shoved up our arses and we were floating—
MICHAEL: And Kate passed me the bottle of vodka. It had her lipstick on
    the rim and it tasted like—
DOM: Sex. All sticky and sweet and burning—
MICHAEL: I was watching your hand run down her hair and over the flesh
    on her back—
DOM: And we were spinning and spinning and spinning. Faster and faster
    and faster—
MICHAEL: It was like I was watching the whole thing from outside my
    own body looking back at myself—
DOM: Faster and faster and faster and I slammed on the brakes—
MICHAEL: And the clear sky lit up with all those stars—

DOM: Spinning and spinning and spinning—

MICHAEL: And then—literally—I was on the outside of the car on someone's lawn.

DOM: And then I was dead.

MICHAEL: And then you were dead. [*To audience*] And that's how it happened. It was like really the most beautiful thing … I never thought anything bad could happen here and then it did.

> KATE *walks slowly off the stage without acknowledging either of them.* DOM *puts on a hospital gown and heads towards a hospital bed. Lights out.*

SCENE SIX

The scene is characterised by quiet and stillness. MICHAEL *is sitting on stage on top of a bed in a hospital gown. Hazy words cascade across the screens. Sometimes they go really quickly. Sometimes they slow down. Sometimes there are a lot of words and sometimes only very few. 'Dom is Smiling' is suspended clearly there for a little while as are phrases like 'Heavy', 'Sorry', 'Concrete'.* MUM *is standing away from the hospital bed looking off in the opposite direction.* POPPY *is holding a helium balloon that says 'Get Well Soon', and staring off into the audience. There is a pervasive sense of awkwardness as though no-one knows how to stand or what to say.* LEENA *is standing near* MICHAEL. DOM *is standing behind* MUM. *No-one notices he is there except for* MICHAEL. *They look at each other for a while from a distance.*

As the lights slowly return, MUM *speaks the following line, becoming louder and more distressed until the last 'no' is said much louder and affirmatively. Perhaps she is spotlighted.*

MUM: No no no no no no no no no no no no no no!

MICHAEL: [*to* MUM] I want to tell you sorry … but the words get stuck inside my throat.

> MUM *doesn't respond.* DOM *walks towards her.*

It's like I've got this concrete in my chest and I'll never really be able to stand straight again with the weight of it.

> LEENA *puts her hand on him.*

I … it … I was on the outside.

LEENA: Shhh … you don't have to talk.

MICHAEL: I … looked back and there—

LEENA: Shhh…

MICHAEL: [*to audience*] If I could just find the right words … I could store our grief in them. I could let them go out of my mouth and into the air.

> MICHAEL *rips* POPPY'*s helium balloon out of his hand and lets it go. He walks offstage.*

END OF ACT ONE

ACT TWO

SCENE ONE

There are the loud background sounds of a school. A couple of SCHOOL-BOYS *at desks jostle each other and talk and carry on loudly. As* MICHAEL *walks out to the centre of the stage in his school uniform everything suddenly goes completely silent.* KATE *stands in a corner of the stage, away from the main action, looking forlorn and with her hair cut.*

MICHAEL: [*to the audience*] First day back at school after the holidays. Next term.

> *The two* SCHOOLBOYS *stop talking and pretend to be really interested in the chewing gum under their desks or their nails or some other insignificant object.* MICHAEL *pauses to look at them briefly. He then climbs into the car, takes out a piece of paper and begins to write but can't. He screws up the piece of paper, throws it away and puts his headphones on. The sound of knocking on a door.*

TEACHER: This is the third lesson in a row. We do have recess and lunch for that sort of thing. You need to go again? I'm sending one of the boys into the toilets to get you if you don't come back in five … Do you need to tell me something?

> MICHAEL *stares off into the distance for a while before taking his headphones off.* DOM *walks up to* KATE *and fondles her hair sadly.*

MICHAEL: What I want to say … is a lot of things. Lots of stories I could tell. Like how Dom's old girlfriend used to have huge-arse hair but now she's cut it off so that she looks all fierce. I saw her at the shops the other day, she's like the kids at school. She doesn't look at me anymore, not now. Not since the funeral. Not since she cried so hard her father had to carry her out of the church. She was just staring at a rack of chips. We were so close and I wanted to go up and touch her and tell her I'm sorry, I'm sorry all the time. But whenever I see her, I can't look her straight in the face. I can't even say her name.

> *A school bell rings.* MICHAEL *puts his headphones on, crawls out*

of the car and walks over to where POPPY *sits on a plastic chair with a transistor radio, sipping a beer and looking off into the distance. The faint sound of horseraces can be heard. There are images of some of the fibro houses and older buildings around Parramatta on the screens, paired with images of construction.*

MICHAEL *sits on a chair next to* POPPY *with his headphones on.* POPPY *looks at him with a hugely exaggerated smile but doesn't get any kind of reaction.* POPPY *gets frustrated and takes* MICHAEL'*s headphones off before smiling at him again.*

Stop! You look like a … like a … like a tool.

POPPY: What, like a bandsaw or a screwdriver?

MICHAEL: Ahh … fuck!

POPPY: I've never heard you use language like that—

MICHAEL: Yeah, well. Everything is changed now. Everything is different.

POPPY: Everyone is trying their best … How's your mum?

MICHAEL *doesn't respond.*

MICHAEL: I can't see what's so interesting about all this.

He gestures toward the foreground.

Why do you want to watch all these old buildings being torn down all the time?

POPPY *looks excitedly off into the distance and does not notice that* DOM *is also counting down with him.*

POPPY: Five, four, three, two, one …

A crashing sound.

Down!

DOM *sits on a plastic chair beside* POPPY.

MICHAEL: Where are all the other old people?

POPPY: Too boring. They stay back inside the retirement home.

He points behind him.

Too much excitement for them out here.

MICHAEL: Watching all those old houses explode …

POPPY: Dom used to like it. Pissed him off though, that they put tents around the houses before they blow them up. He wanted to watch fibro blow up into the air and land all over the place.

MICHAEL: I remember that bloke who lived here had all those pigeons.

Pigeons fly around the screens. DOM *looks at them delightedly.*

POPPY: That was fantastic. They were homing pigeons. Him and a couple of other blokes down the road used to let 'em go at the same time and see whose pigeons could get back the fastest.

MICHAEL: Don't see that stuff anymore.

POPPY: That Parramatta got lost in those tall buildings …

MICHAEL: Can't remember what it looked like.

POPPY: I do. I remember it as clear as if it was in front of me. That's why you keep on telling stories. So the memories never go away.

MICHAEL: So you remember.

POPPY: Exactly.

MICHAEL: Everything is changed now.

There is a long pause. DOM *and* MICHAEL *stare at each other in recognition that they are not just talking about the landscape.*

POPPY: But you can still tell the story of when everything was different.

SCENE TWO

SHADI *and* MICHAEL *enter in their swimmers.* SHADI *has bags of groceries and coolers in his arms. He has too much food. He struggles to carry everything. They sit down beside the pool. One of the screens displays the image of a 'pool'. The sign says: 'No Diving, No Running, No Eating in the Pool'. Underneath the instructions 'No Rangas' has been written in and crossed out, 'No Asians with gangsta tattoos' has been written in and crossed out, 'No fat chicks' has been written in underneath. It is not crossed out.* MICHAEL *and* SHADI *pass food and drinks back and forth.* DOM *drops a bikini top from the diving board.*

SHADI: There's my cousin! And my other cousin and my other cousin … Hope *she's* not my cousin!

He tries to give MICHAEL *a high five but he is unresponsive.*

Ay, bro, she's lookin' at you. Nah, nah, look, she looked this way. Yeah, maybe. Yeah, no. She's looking at you. Nah, she looked. It was just for a second but like she definitely looked at ya, bro.

He jostles MICHAEL *and tries to get him to be more responsive.*

Nah. Nah. I think you're right. She must be looking at me. You too ugly, bro.

MICHAEL: You going in?

SHADI: Nah, think I need to, you know, eat another sandwich. Get my strength up first.

MICHAEL: Shadi, your mum packs too many snacks.

SHADI: It's mostly for you. You're my best friend and she worries that your mum might forget to feed ya.

MICHAEL: I can feed myself.

SHADI: Yeah but, bro. You know.

> SHADI *takes a sandwich and stands up. The bikini top grabs his attention and he moves towards it. He picks it up. He's delighted.* SAL *enters hesitantly, covering her breasts.* SHADI *stands there with the bikini top and the sandwich and stares.*

SAL: Excuse me. Is that mine? Did you ... did you get it back for me from those boys?

SHADI: Yes. Yes, I did.

> SAL *turns around so that he can put it on for her. There is some awkward fumbling between the sandwich and bikini top before she turns around again.*

You want a cupcake?

SAL: Yeah.

> SAL *and* SHADI *return to* MICHAEL *and the food.* MICHAEL *snaps out of his daydreaming and stares at* SAL.

SHADI: So my mum packed chocolate cupcakes, or strawberry ones or chips ...

> *As he turns around to* SAL *with armfuls of food he is suddenly pushed over by two* BOYS *who run past. Food explodes everywhere.*

SAL: Are you alright?

> SHADI *doesn't respond.*

Do you need CPR?

SHADI: [*sitting up all of a sudden*] Yes!

SAL: Maybe you just need a hand getting up?

SHADI: I'll take that.

MONIQUE *turns up with a towel wrapped around her and sits next to* MICHAEL. SAL *and* SHADI *flirt with each other.* MICHAEL *watches* SAL *and* SHADI *with a stunned look.* MONIQUE *works on her tan.*

MICHAEL: [*turning to* MONIQUE] Who is that?

MONIQUE: That's my mate Sal.

MICHAEL: And who are you?

MONIQUE: I'm her mate Monique. Mo for short.

MICHAEL: So Shadi's talking to a girl. Like a real live girl.

MONIQUE: That she is.

MICHAEL: And she's talking to Shadi.

MONIQUE: She doesn't have particularly high standards.

MICHAEL: Right. Well, that works then.

MICHAEL: Monique, Mo … I like your dress.

MONIQUE: It's a towel.

MICHAEL: Well, it looks really good on you.

MONIQUE: It's hot. It's so hot today.

She takes a can out of the esky and begins to rub it across her forehead. DOM *puts a Coke in* MICHAEL*'s hand and directs him to* MONIQUE*'s shoulder.* DOM *lets the hand go and* MICHAEL *rubs it down* MONIQUE*'s arm.*

MICHAEL: Here you go.

SCENE THREE

MUM *is alone inside the family apartment. She packs Dom's things into a milk crate. She includes his sweatshirt, his shoes, some pictures.* POPPY *stands away from her, concerned. She does not acknowledge him.*

SCENE FOUR

The family electrical shop. MUM *stands completely still, expressionless, staring out to the audience.* POPPY *and* MICHAEL *unpack boxes.* LEENA *attempts to sell things to customers.*

LEENA: Want to buy a plug? We got Australia-Lebanon, China-Australia. Hey you, you look a bit like an Australia-India guy yourself. Want to buy a plug?

POPPY: [*to* MICHAEL] Big year for you. Just started Year Eleven, you'll
   be doing your HSC soon. Before you know it you'll be going places.
MICHAEL: Don't know how much it matters right now.
POPPY: It matters. You'll go to university. Maybe write a book.
MICHAEL: Or I'll still be here helping out in the family electrical shop.
   Even Aunty Leena's working here now.
POPPY: It's good you're here and Aunty Leena too. Your mother needs
   all of us right now.
MICHAEL: Or she doesn't even know I'm there anymore.
POPPY: She does—
MICHAEL: Or she doesn't care if I am. Hey, Mum. Mum … She's just
   become a part of the wall. Mum … wallpaper.
MUM: Oh, right. Right. You. Morning!
MICHAEL: It's afternoon.
MUM: Oh, I'll make us some sandwiches then.

   MUM *gets out a loaf of bread and a knife and some sandwich
   items but isn't able to complete the task. She appears unable to
   understand how to make a sandwich.*

We could all go out for a walk later.
LEENA: Down by the river. You've always liked it there.

   MUM *talks out loud to no-one in particular. She speaks slowly.
   She is remembering.*

MUM: Down by the river.

   *She begins to pile pieces of bread into a stack on a plate and
   pours something over it so that it is a poor imitation of pancakes.*

The river?
LEENA: Yes the river.
MUM: Where the David Jones is?
LEENA: Not there anymore.
MUM: Right. And the river?
LEENA: Still there.
MUM: And the bench?
LEENA: Still there.
MUM: I carved my name.
LEENA: [*with sadness, faltering a little*] Still there.

MUM *holds the plate out in front of her.* DOM *puts his arm around her.* MICHAEL *stands back and looks at her, his arms wide open and stretched out towards her.* POPPY *puts his hand on* MICHAEL's *back.* LEENA *tries to distract everyone from their sadness by making more jokes about electrical plugs.*

LEENA: Hey you! Wanna buy a plug?

SCENE FIVE

The sounds of the neighbourhood can be heard in the background—sports games at the stadium, chatter, construction, cars. The screens return to images of apartment blocks. SHADI *is dressed in his swimming gear and has some other pool paraphernalia with him. There are a couple of piles of odd junk near the front of the stage. It's council tip day.* POPPY *sits onstage listening to horseraces on his transistor radio.* ESTHER *throws old junk off her balcony. It lands onstage from above.* SHADI *enters. The things* ESTHER *is throwing from the sky narrowly miss him. He looks alarmed and then jovial. He dumps his pool paraphernalia on the ground.*

SHADI: Alright! Council tip day.

He rummages through the piles of junk. POPPY *sits up and begins to pay attention to what* SHADI *is taking and discarding.*

POPPY: Treasure … trash … treasure …

SHADI *opens a box and pulls out a pair of sneakers.* POPPY *hesitates, recognising that they are Dom's, and nods.*

Treasure.

SHADI *flips off his thongs and puts the sneakers on.* ESTHER *appears onstage and moves odd junk around. She is dressed inappropriately for the job.*

Esther! What are you doing?

ESTHER: Getting myself organised, old man.

She looks at POPPY *and then notices* SHADI.

I wouldn't be standing there with no shirt on. Not much to show for it.

She cracks herself up. The sound of banging on a door.

MAN: [*voice-over*] Mum! Let me in!

ESTHER: Gotta go.

ESTHER exits. MICHAEL *enters, walks towards* SHADI *and immediately gets stuck staring at* SHADI*'s shoes, which he also clearly recognises as being Dom's.*

SHADI: I thought we were going to the pool today.

It is clear that MICHAEL *has forgotten. He looks disoriented and confused.*

MICHAEL: Those shoes.

DOM: Treasure!

MICHAEL: They look like sneakers that used to belong to …

He trails off and gets lost in his own thoughts.

SHADI: Maybe we could skip the pool today? Maybe we just hang out together? We could go have a walk or talk or not talk or you could just continue standing there looking like crap or whatever, whatever you need to do.

He picks up a couch cushion from the pile and hangs it up from some part of the stage so that it is suspended in the air. He begins to hit it like he is boxing. He is clumsy and uncoordinated. He encourages MICHAEL *to do the same.* MICHAEL *just stares at him.* SHADI *boxes badly and hands out philosophical advice while doing so.*

You see. Mohammed Ali says the way you hit can show what sort of person you are; it shows if you're not sure enough about yourself, if you've got too much anger, if you're the sort of person who gets knocked over and never gets up again.

He continues boxing. He puts all of his effort into it but he's not very skilled.

You have to breathe … breathe …

MUM *walks towards the front of the stage and picks up a large box of things in the council tip pile. She puts it back again. She picks it up. She puts it back. She looks at* SHADI*'s shoes. She addresses* SHADI*'s feet in a flat tone.*

MUM: Those are his shoes. They're his.

She picks up the box again and moves away from SHADI *and* MICHAEL, *who observe her in silence.* SHADI *quietly slips off the shoes and leaves them on stage.* MUM *takes items out of the box, examining each piece carefully. She smiles sometimes.* DOM *passes her the things from the box. She takes them without acknowledging him. There are more signs of life in her than we have seen previously. She pulls out the type of things one can throw away—sweatshirts, worn sneakers, et cetera.*

MICHAEL: [*looking towards* MUM] She's got Dom in a box again.

He punches, stops, looks at her again and then walks slowly toward her.

Mum … Mum …

She is unresponsive. MICHAEL *lays a hand on her shoulder—there seems to be some recognition of him standing there.*

It's just. We've got so many other things of his. Just throw this lot away …

MICHAEL *tries to pack the things away but* MUM *pulls them out again.*

MUM: Tell me the story.

She holds out an old sweatshirt

MICHAEL: Alright, alright.

DOM *puts the sweatshirt on.*

Here he is, wearing this old thing on the football field. Dom with his electric blue eyes popping out of his head like someone's plugged him in. He looks like he's about to launch himself out of that football field and into the street where the cars are waiting for him … [*To the audience*] Mum wouldn't have a clue about him really, about why her good china pot went missing or about all those *Playboys* he buried in the front yard of our apartment block. And now she's stuck inside a box with him …

POPPY: She'll do what she needs to do …

MICHAEL, *growing frustrated, walks over to the makeshift punching bag* SHADI *has set up and begins punching.*

MICHAEL: She doesn't even know I'm here.

MUM *breaks out of her haze momentarily and looks at* MICHAEL.

MUM: [*muttering*] You … you … you … I do know.

SHADI: [*unsure*] Come on. Let's go. We could go for a walk. Maybe go to the pool.

MUM: [*angry, but unsure of herself*] You're there. You're leaving?

MICHAEL: Going out.

MUM: Where?

MICHAEL: Out.

MUM *picks up Dom's shoes and looks off into the distance.*

MUM: Stay.

DOM *walks slowly out onto the stage and puts his hand on his mother's back. She doesn't acknowledge his presence.* MICHAEL *returns to boxing, hitting the bag as hard as he can.*

SCENE SIX

A flashing sign, 'Fruit and Vegetables', appears on the screen. MONIQUE *unpacks and arranges boxes of fruit.* MICHAEL *helps her. He is a bit awkward. She is very confident.* MONIQUE'S DAD *sits in the corner, smoking a shisha pipe, relaxing but clearly watching every move* MICHAEL *makes with his daughter.*

MICHAEL: You smell like fruit.

MONIQUE: Yeah well, I live above a fruit shop. We all smell like fruit. Most days we go to the markets first thing in the morning when you get the fresh stuff and then again in the afternoon when it's cheap and you get all the bargains. My younger brother Joe, he's literally a fruit cake. He goes to your school. He knows you.

MICHAEL: Joe?

MONIQUE: Year Eight. The boys are always throwing him in the garbage can.

MICHAEL: Oh, Joe …

He makes some kind of effeminate gesture with his hands.

MONIQUE: Hey, stop it! Yeah, that's my brother.

MICHAEL: Isn't he that kid that was on the front page of the *Daily Telegraph*?

MONIQUE: Oh, man. We don't talk about that anymore. My father was sooooo pissed! [*Imitating her brother Joe*] In the Western Suburbs guns are easier to get than pizzas! [*Returning to her own voice*] You know, my dad said he had to play football, so he joins this team and their first game is in Lakemba the day after some totally random shooting happened. So anyways, the team benched him the whole time, of course, so he wanders off to get a slice of pizza from some corner store and runs into this reporter who's interviewing people. I think she was like the only person who paid attention to him that day, so he gave her what she wanted.

MICHAEL: I've only seen your dad from a distance ... outside ... smoking that stuff that smells like apples ...

MONIQUE: Yeah, shisha. Him and all his other Egyptian mates ...

MICHAEL: He looks a little frightening ...

MONIQUE: [*imitating her father*] My son, he is number one football player! [*Returning to herself*] They're just smoking stuff that smells like apples and telling each other lies like men in every other place do.

MICHAEL: Bit of a different kind of guy than your brother?

MONIQUE: Yeah, Dad desperately wants Joe to learn how to play football. I try to teach him, but you know ...

She imitates Joe and begins to try and handle a football. She trips and misses and catches it in a comical manner. She runs into MICHAEL *who picks her up again. They stand close together in an intimate gesture and it looks like they might kiss until* MONIQUE'S DAD *stares at them and coughs.* MONIQUE *speaks in a very abrupt and matter-of-fact way.*

So how exactly did your brother die? Was it in the actual car or like later in the hospital? Did you see it? Did you see him die like right there next to you?

MICHAEL *touches* MONIQUE *on the arm as though considering how to answer and then begins to speak. A clam night sky is played on the back screens.* DOM *emerges from the side of the stage.*

MICHAEL: No ... not exactly. I just saw the night sky and his hand running through his girlfriend's hair—

DOM: Spinning and spinning and spinning—

MICHAEL: As if the future would just keep coming—

DOM: All sticky and sweet and burning—

MICHAEL: But I saw him again the next day. I never told anyone this, but I saw him when I was in the hospital. I knew it was Dom by the way he tilted his head slightly to the left and tucked his hands into the pockets of his saggy jeans.

> DOM *and* MICHAEL *stare at each other.* DOM *shoves his hands in his pockets but does not leave.*

I could see he wasn't offering any kind of sadness … he was just saying goodbye.

> *The Pontiac Trans Am appears and disappears across the three screens at the back.*

MONIQUE: So he was here and then not here.

MICHAEL: Here. Not here.

MONIQUE: But right now we're here in my parents' fruit shop.

MICHAEL: Incredible.

END OF ACT TWO

ACT THREE

SCENE ONE

Images of North Parramatta McDonald's parking lot at night appear on the screen. MICHAEL, SHADI, MONIQUE *and* SAL *lie around and on top of the car eating McDonald's. They chat and point at the other kids in the parking lot breakdancing and carrying on.*

SAL: Shadi, Shadi, can we get inside the car for a little bit?

SHADI: Nup. The twenty dollars I gave my cousin only covers us for sitting on the outside of his car. If we get inside I'm guaranteed to lose my nut sack. He's up at the club down the street—

MICHAEL: And because the bouncers are dicks at One World and Collectors—

SHADI: Yeah. That's where we should be. I look eighteen. Don't know why they won't let me in.

MICHAEL: And the parks are full of dodgies and Westfield is shut at night …

MONIQUE: McDonald's is the centre of our night-time universe … at least for now.

MICHAEL: Or maybe not!

> MONIQUE *hands* MICHAEL *a pair of pliers. The screen returns to the local swimming pool.* MICHAEL *assists the others to break in by pulling back the wire fence. They are all hesitant at first but then joyful and excited about what they have done.* SHADI *and* SAL *flirt, talk and play, while* MICHAEL *and* MONIQUE *become the focus of the action.*

[*To* MONIQUE] What are you thinking?

MONIQUE: That's what everyone asks you!

MICHAEL: I wanted to be the first one in for once.

> *He fidgets and looks around.*

It's so quiet.

MONIQUE: So not like daytime.

MICHAEL: It's like a whole 'nother universe in here. Night-time. Shame I didn't bring my swimmers.

> MONIQUE *slowly begins to remove her clothes until she is left wearing only yellow underwear and a bra.* MICHAEL *hesitantly touches her arm.*

You look like butter underneath your clothes.

> *They almost kiss.*

MONIQUE: Fuck!

> *Spotlights circle around the stage.* SAL *and* SHADI *scream and giggle and run around the stage barely dressed. A* SECURITY GUARD *appears.* MONIQUE *distracts him.*

Hey! Hey! Over here!

> MICHAEL *hesitates to run off but* SAL *and* SHADI *grab him and drag him off.*

SCENE TWO

It's morning. MICHAEL *is at home. He walks across the stage in his school uniform carrying and spilling objects—his jacket, cereal, pens and books—everywhere. He is distracted and dreamy but clearly happy thinking about what happened with* MONIQUE *the night before.* MUM *is already onstage.* LEENA *and* POPPY *enter.* POPPY *gets himself a coffee and also makes a mess.* MICHAEL *walks around, still dreamy and muttering.*

MICHAEL: Yellow, underwear, skin, all that skin, warm, swimming, taking off her clothes.
LEENA: Here to take you to school, kiddo.

> MICHAEL *does not acknowledge her.*

Ay, you! You've got sex in your head, I can see it. You're just like your brother. He had sex on the brain too, I think it made him a bit retarded.

> MUM *starts to clean and pick things up off the floor but pauses abruptly on hearing* LEENA*'s statement about her son.*

MUM: [*to* LEENA] He wasn't retarded.

> *She continues to clean. Suddenly she grabs something heavy and*

throws it to the ground/walls. POPPY, LEENA *and* MICHAEL *stop and look at her, startled.*

LEENA: Hun, hun. You alright? What do you want? What can I get you?

MUM *picks up a basket of laundry and throws it everywhere. She grows increasingly hysterical.*

MUM: [*looking at* MICHAEL] I want you to do your own laundry …

She picks up his cereal bowl and throws it against the wall.

And to pick up after yourself.

She looks at POPPY.

And I want you to stop spilling your damn beer and your damn coffee all over my floor.

She pours drinks and coffee all over the place.

And you …

She looks at LEENA *and pauses for a moment.*

You do whatever you want to do anyway.

She continues throwing and destroying things. LEENA *and* POPPY *stare at her.*

MICHAEL: [*to* MUM] What you want is to start the story all over, to go back to the beginning again, before ice skating, before cars, before school, before summer holidays.

The same sound of an engine revving that began the play sounds again. The screens play pre-recorded footage of the opening scene. Perhaps it plays a bit and then is rewound so that we can see the 'rewinding.' MUM *stops what she is doing and looks up to the screen.* MICHAEL *looks at* DOM. POPPY *and* LEENA *clean.*

You want to go back to when Dom was just the biggest guy in the school. Best car in the West. When he said he was named after Dominic Toretto from *The Fast and The Furious* movies and he walked around the place like he owned it.

DOM *climbs into the car. He is relishing the chance to drive again.*

For those ten seconds or less.

DOM: I am free.

SCENE THREE

MICHAEL *is in his school uniform. He is walking to school with* POPPY.
The screens slowly fill up with liquid Coke. POPPY *follows slightly
behind. They walk slowly.* DOM *is still sitting in the car.* MICHAEL *stands
still and stares into the distance.* POPPY *gradually walks up beside him.*

MICHAEL: I know you're there. I can see you, you know.
POPPY: [*with a shrug*] Always going to be here.
MICHAEL: I'm too old to be walked to school. Everyone can see you.
POPPY: But I want to talk to you.
MICHAEL: About what?
POPPY: Anything.

> *A school bell rings. There is the sound of kids in the distance.* JOE
> *runs by and pushes against* MICHAEL*'s arm.*

JOE: Your Aunty Leena's a MILF!

> JOE *runs off.*

MICHAEL: I'm sixteen.
POPPY: You're not going anywhere very fast.
MICHAEL: I like it here, in front of this …
POPPY: Old Coke factory.
MICHAEL: You don't understand.
POPPY: Remember I used to walk you by here when you were children?
   They used to have that bloke in a little shop at the front and I'd buy you
   both soda and lollipops. Now, no shop. All these vending machines—
MICHAEL: You don't understand anything.
POPPY: I'm trying to understand. I'm trying to understand a lot of things,
   just like you. It's hard for everyone. Adults too. He was my grandson
   and your mum, she's my daughter you know, my child. It helps to
   keep telling the stories.
MICHAEL: The story here …

> MICHAEL *hesitates.*

POPPY: If anyone can tell it, it's you.
MICHAEL: The story in this place …

> *He pauses.* POPPY *puts a hand on his shoulder.* DOM *looks towards
> the Coke factory and quietly sings a few lines from their ads.*

Dom and me, we used to come here before school and stare through that fence. Dom had big dreams of breaking in one day, of scaling the walls of its giant rectangular surfaces and diving into a giant sea of Coke. If I stand here long enough it's like I can feel him, like he's here. I close my eyes and I picture him somewhere in those big grey buildings, floating in the bubbling brown liquid, Coke bleeding through his thick hair.

POPPY *seems to notice for the first time that* DOM *is there. He falls to his knees and begins to sob.*

END OF ACT THREE

ACT FOUR

SHADI *and* MICHAEL *are sitting on two plastic chairs at the front of the stage.* SHADI *is facing backwards, drawing something on his chair that the audience can't see. They are amongst other* SCHOOLBOYS *at a school assembly. The* PRINCIPAL *is speaking to the assembly. His words are muffled but loud. There are random snatches of clearly articulated words. He looks like he is so passionate and amused by his own speech that he doesn't really care what the students are doing.*

PRINCIPAL: Responsibility ... Actions ... Behaviours ...

> *The* SCHOOLBOYS *call back and forth throughout the* PRINCIPAL*'s speech.*

SCHOOLBOYS: Butt pirate! Sausage jockey! Queen! Faggot!

MICHAEL: School assembly. There's nothing else for the boys to do but draw dicks on chairs.

> SHADI *turns the chair around and proudly lifts it up to show the audience the giant dick he has drawn there.*

And call each other gay.

> JOE *enters, followed by the sound of laughter. He screams at someone offstage and gestures in an effeminate manner.*

JOE: Why you got to touch my stuff? You fruit fairy sodomite butt-pirate queen.

MICHAEL: [*putting his head in his hands*] Oh, God!

SHADI: He's like someone from a Beyoncé video clip.

JOE: [*pointing at someone in the audience*] Hey you! Sausage jockey!

MICHAEL: That's Monique's brother.

> SHADI *is piecing things together and offers the following words as if they are a revelation to him.*

SHADI: So, to stop everyone from calling him gay, he makes sure he picks on other people before they pick on him. Amazing. I keep thinking of what Mo did that night at the pool. She's got bigger balls than any of us ... and that's her brother.

MICHAEL: Yep.

He grabs JOE *and forces him into the chair next to him.*

Sit. Alright. Just shut up and people won't bother you.

JOE: Yeah, that's right. I'm sitting over here now, with all my friends in Year Eleven! [*To* SHADI] What up, homo?

SHADI: Shut up.

JOE leans back in his chair, cowering.

PRINCIPAL: And no-one will be going to that riot in Harris Park!

SHADI and MICHAEL jump up excitedly. JOE jumps up after they do.

MICHAEL, SHADI & JOE: [*together*] A riot in Harris Park!

They run off and then return to climb on top of the car and stand on it watching the action. JOE *is thoroughly enjoying the scene.* MICHAEL *and* SHADI *look less sure. A* POLICE RIOT SQUAD OFFICER *moves to the front of the stage, facing away from the audience, 'Riot Squad' on the back of their jacket. There is the sound of someone giving a lecture in Hindi.*

JOE: Alright! Lebs versus Indians!

SHADI: Doesn't look as good as the Cronulla one …

MICHAEL: Looked bigger on the TV …

SHADI: Just all those guys in riot gear.

MICHAEL: Like a promise no-one's keeping.

INDIAN WOMAN: It is not a riot. It is a debate. This is important in a democracy. We must protest for our right—

A JOURNALIST *enters and stands at the front of the stage with a microphone like he is addressing a camera.*

JOURNALIST: Here in 'The Suburb that Simmers' Indian students say they are routinely attacked by Lebanese men at the train station. When a rumour circulated last night that recent attacks on two local businesses and the firebombing of an Indian student house were also perpetrated by young men of Lebanese ethnicity the local Indian community, mostly the students, took over the roundabout on Wigram Street to protest the lack of police action.

LEBANESE MAN: A hundred and fifty Indians came after three young Lebanese boys with hockey sticks and crowbars.

MICHAEL *puts his hands in his pockets and turns his hat backwards like Dom.*

MICHAEL: Shadi, I don't know if I like it as much as I thought I would.

JOE *observes* MICHAEL *and tries to be more serious. He imitates* MICHAEL*'s look.*

SHADI: Me neither.

MICHAEL *starts to realise that* JOE *is imitating him.*

MICHAEL: It's like when those Sudanese kids showed up at school—

SHADI: Because their county fell apart or something.

MICHAEL: And no-one knew how to be friendly.

LEBANESE MAN: I don't care where you all come from! All these young idiots! The police should let me slap them upside the head so I can get back to my shop!

JOE: Ay, youse pooftas … ahhh …

SHADI *and* MICHAEL *give him the evil eye. He begins to mumble and is unsure of what to say.*

Youse just be friendly to one another!

MICHAEL *and* SHADI *nod to show their approval.* JOE *gains confidence and speaks louder.*

Yeah like, love one another and all that, alright?

The JOURNALIST *walks towards* JOE *and holds a microphone out in front of him.*

JOURNALIST: And what do you think about what you've seen here today young man?

JOE: In the western suburbs it's easier to …

He looks at MICHAEL.

… be kind than get a pizza.

POPPY *creeps out from the side of the stage and watches them. They climb off the car and walk off in his direction.*

END OF ACT FOUR

ACT FIVE

SCENE ONE

The 'Fruit and Vegetables' sign flashes on the screen. MONIQUE *and* MICHAEL*'s bodies are close together and there are intimate gestures shared between and around their talking.* MONIQUE *is holding a bunch of grapes, which she flings about excitedly as she talks.*

MONIQUE: So we went to see a riot too, but it wasn't actually happening now, but it was so amazing when it did happen back then in the sixties or something. Our teacher explained it. In that place they call the Parramatta Girls' Home down by the river where they put all those girls they thought didn't behave very ladylike. These girls, they got so angry because they were being abused in there and all and no-one listened to them when they complained, so they climbed up on top of the roof of the building and they grabbed all the tiles off one by one and they [*Beginning to re-enact this by picking off grapes and throwing them*] threw them down at the guards below. And later, because they wouldn't say sorry, the people who ran the place wouldn't put the roof tiles back on, so the girls had to sleep there all through winter, the rain and all coming down through the ceiling, and they only had these crappy thin pyjamas.

MICHAEL: That's not the same …

MONIQUE: It is the same. Just people wanting people to listen to them, to hear their stories. There's stories everywhere in this neighbourhood. You know that, you know more than anybody. I've seen you, writing stories down all the time.

MICHAEL *looks fidgety.* DOM *shows up and starts egging him on.*

DOM: Touch her. Go on. Touch her.

MONIQUE: Are you listening to me?

MICHAEL: Yes! I just find it hard, sometimes, to understand everything you're saying when I'm looking at you at the same time.

MONIQUE: Tell me a story then.

MICHAEL *takes a piece of paper out of his pocket and reads from it.*

MICHAEL: Dom takes us out past Granville—

MONIQUE: What about a different story, like maybe something that's not about Dom?

> MICHAEL *takes other pieces of paper out of his pockets/shirt, looks at them, and looks up at Dom. He crumples up the pieces of paper and throws them on the floor. He takes the original story back out of his pocket again, unfolds it and gives* MONIQUE *some kind of apologetic gesture.*

MICHAEL: We drive … late afternoon … after school … Auburn … past—

> DOM *stands over his shoulder and reads for him.*

DOM: The dusty little storefronts and factories long since shut down, past the hairdressers with their old-man customers and the women with their eighties freestyle hair, past the shops with their naked plastic mannequins looking like sex.

> DOM *moves back and lets* MICHAEL *continue.* MICHAEL *gets into it, enjoying the story more. He looks at* DOM *as he reads.*

MICHAEL: Dom … Dom has one hand on the wheel and his head stuck out the window so that his thick hair flies back like he's in a tunnel. I tell myself that we are kings of these neighbourhoods, driving through with our big fancy car, checking out what our people are doing. I watch Dom smiling his gigantic full-of-teeth smile and I know that he is dreaming the same thing and he sticks his head out the window again …

> MONIQUE *steps in front of* MICHAEL, *cutting off the gaze between the brothers and forcing* MICHAEL *to look at her.*

And I drag him back into the big safety of that car.

> MICHAEL *pulls* MONIQUE *towards him.* MONIQUE'S DAD *looks into the room and says something to* MONIQUE *in Arabic.*

MONIQUE'S DAD: [*to* MICHAEL] You! Get out!

SCENE TWO

MICHAEL *is down at the Parramatta River. He runs his fingers over the place where his mother carved her name.* DOM *sits beside* MICHAEL, *who does not notice him.* DOM *runs his hand across the carved name too.*

SCENE THREE

MUM *enters and sits with her box of Dom's things. She looks at objects and pieces of paper she draws out of the box.* MICHAEL *looks at her from afar. He looks frustrated.*

MICHAEL: Sometimes I don't know if I can take any more of her silence.

> SHADI *enters. He pulls the couch cushion along behind him and then hoists it up.*

SHADI: [*to* MICHAEL, *who follows his instructions*] Uppercut, uppercut, jab, cross, repeat, uppercut, uppercut, uppercut …

> *He works* MICHAEL *so hard he starts to falter and gets out of breath, but* SHADI *pushes him further.*

Again, again, again …

> MICHAEL *pauses to look at* MUM *again.*

Mohammed Ali says you can't give everything away at once, you've got to hold back a little, keep something in reserve.

> MICHAEL *walks closer to his mother but keeps his distance. He looks at her. She knows he's there and is made uncomfortable by his presence. She doesn't acknowledge his presence.*

MICHAEL: [*to* MUM] I went down to the river the other day, you know, where you carved your name into that bench, all that time ago, before Dom and I were born, before cars and ice skating and everything else. You put it there, so that you would always know where you came from, so you would always know how to get back here.

> MUM *doesn't respond.* MICHAEL *wrestles the box of things away from her.* LEENA *shows up and gives it back to her.*

[*To* LEENA, *with frustration*] She's stuck!

LEENA: [*intimately*] Sometimes you need something to pour your grief into … Where's the girl?

MICHAEL: Not allowed out.

LEENA: Why?

MICHAEL: Her father says she can't be trusted with me.

LEENA: Is he the guy who's always sitting out front smoking that stuff that smells like apples?

MICHAEL: Uh-huh.

LEENA *smiles.*

SCENE FOUR

MICHAEL *is back at home in his apartment block. There are images of apartment blocks on the back screens.* ESTHER *enters, dragging paint tins around with difficulty.*

MICHAEL: Esther, let me help you.
ESTHER: Thanks.
MICHAEL: What are you doing with all this paint?
ESTHER: We're going to paint. We're starting fresh.
MICHAEL: You and who?
ESTHER: My son.
MICHAEL: Your son?
ESTHER: He's back.
MICHAEL: I've heard him come back before.
ESTHER: But he's a better kind of back now.
MICHAEL: Are you sure?
ESTHER: Never can be.
MICHAEL: But you're starting things again, you're going to paint.
ESTHER: I put my best frock on.
MICHAEL: Good idea.
ESTHER: For the occasion.

She begins to walk away.

Oh, there was a girl here for you.
MICHAEL: When?
ESTHER: A little while ago. She was just sitting there by the mailboxes looking up to your apartment. I asked her if she was looking for you.
MICHAEL: What did she say?
ESTHER: She said she wasn't sure.
MICHAEL: Not sure of what?
ESTHER: Not sure if she was looking for you or not.
MICHAEL: But how come she's not sure?
ESTHER: How should I know? Why don't you just go get her?
MICHAEL: Go get her?

ESTHER: Well you're clearly after her.

MICHAEL: [*thinking it over*] Yeah go get her … you know if I were to write your story maybe I'd call it 'Hope.'

ESTHER: As long as you call me Marilyn, like Marilyn Monroe.

MICHAEL: What?

ESTHER: Well if Dom got to be Dominic Toretto. I should get to be Marilyn.

MICHAEL: That doesn't make any sense.

ESTHER: Nothing ever does.

She walks offstage. From afar she shouts, 'Go get her!'

SCENE FIVE

The 'Fruit and Vegetables' sign flashes. MICHAEL *looks up to where* MONIQUE *is looking out the window above her parents' shop. She listens to some kind of aggressive music and looks sad and frustrated. She writes things down on a pad of paper and throws them out the window.* MICHAEL *picks them up and reads the content aloud as she throws them down.*

MICHAEL: [*reading*] 'Go away. My father says no, I can't be with you anymore …' [*To* MONIQUE] But … what if we just don't tell him?

MONIQUE *throws down another note which he picks up and reads.*

[*Reading*] 'He'll know. He always knows.'

SCENE SIX

Images of Parramatta flash on the screen. MICHAEL *walks the streets.*

MICHAEL: Inside our apartment now, there's so much silence. I like it out here. Where things are louder. That's what this place is. Shiny cars and loud things, people coming, people going. Movement. It helps me think.

He's walking around town thinking. He climbs into the car. DOM *is already sitting there.* MICHAEL *doesn't acknowledge him.*

[*Slowly, contemplative*] I have this dream where Dom is here. He's all see-through like a ghost and he's got this glow about him like a tail-light. I say to him, 'Drive'.

DOM: [*slowly, contemplative*] We are glowing purple. We speed up and break, sliding over concrete—

MICHAEL: Like primo-star ice skaters, Dom with his arm hanging out the window, scanning for girls, and me trying to look all relaxed like I'm him, like I'm ready for the world to just keep coming and coming, Dom by my side again.

Turns and faces DOM.

But you're not are you?

DOM: What?

MICHAEL: You're not really there are you?

DOM smiles and puts his arm around MICHAEL *as if he is about to speak but just then* JOE *enters the stage, making a lot of noise. They both watch him. He is playing with a football and handling it very badly. He moves clumsily and comically.* MICHAEL *gets out of the car and watches him for a bit before going over to demonstrate how to kick the ball around.*

I'll help you …

JOE: Don't know if I can be helped.

MICHAEL: Don't know if you can be helped either …

MONIQUE'S DAD *enters unnoticed.*

JOE: The boys at school, they call me—

MICHAEL: I know … But maybe if I could show you some moves—

JOE: You could show me?

JOE and MICHAEL *both observe that* MONIQUE'S DAD *is there watching them.* MONIQUE'S DAD *gives* MICHAEL *an angry look for a moment as though he's going to tell him to get lost.*

MICHAEL: I could try.

He demonstrates how to do things. MONIQUE'S DAD *relaxes a little. Folds his arms and watches.*

I'll give it my best shot.

JOE: Great!

MICHAEL: You can maybe hang around me. Maybe—

JOE: Yeah? I can hang out with you?

MONIQUE'S DAD stares. MICHAEL *stares back.*

MICHAEL: Yeah. You can hang around me when you need to. I can teach you, you know football and lots of other stuff.

SCENE SEVEN

The street outside the apartment building. MUM *enters. There is an awkward moment where she catches* MICHAEL'*s eyes.*

MUM: Where are you going?
MICHAEL: Out … I mean if that's alright. I was going over to Shadi's.
MUM: It's alright. I mean you should go out. That's what you do … that's … that's what young people do.

MICHAEL *nods and walks over closer towards* MUM.

Can I take you there?
MICHAEL: Sure. That'd be great.

They get into the car but don't go anywhere.

MUM: What are you two up to tonight?
MICHAEL: We're just going out to one of those charcoal chicken places near Shadi's in Granville.
MUM: Dom used to say night-time—
MUM & MICHAEL: [*together*] Is what charcoal chicken is made for.
MICHAEL: Yeah, those were the best times. When we'd just stop and eat and there was silence between us and I knew that everything was good.
MUM: I found a photograph of you two on his phone. You both had these mad smiles and chicken sandwiches in your hands and … a bright glow on Dom's face. Like headlights. Like he was something holy.
MICHAEL: Dom used to say this place is made of cars and charcoal chicken and God.
MUM: You have to know that sometimes when I'm not talking I'm just trying to find him again, to remember everything he was in that silent space, like you say, where everything is good.
MICHAEL: Does it work? Do you find him there?
MUM: I try. Sometimes I think I find him there and then I lose him again.

ESTHER *walks up to the car window and knocks on it, holding out a box of biscuits.*

ESTHER: Hey, Michael? I bought you those biscuits.

MUM: [*a statement, not a question*] You bring my son biscuits.

ESTHER: He's writing me a story.

MUM: You're writing Esther a story?

> MICHAEL *takes a bite of a biscuit, but clearly doesn't enjoy it.*

MICHAEL: Maybe.

MUM: I haven't seen you writing.

MICHAEL: Poppy gave me a new notebook.

> *He takes it out and holds it up to her. She takes it and turns it around in her hands before passing it back.*

MUM: [*to* ESTHER] He's writing you a story?

> *There is an awkward pause as* MUM *stares out into the distance.*

MICHAEL: What are you doing, Esther?

ESTHER: Waiting.

MICHAEL: For what?

ESTHER: My son.

MICHAEL: I thought he was back.

ESTHER: He is back. Back and then not back. That's just what it's like. Being a mother. You spend a lifetime waiting.

MUM: And sometimes they don't come back.

ESTHER: No. They always come back in some way or another. And how are you travelling Susan?

> MUM *does not respond. She looks like she is trying to find the right words but can't.* MICHAEL *pulls her gently out of the car.*

MICHAEL: Shadi can wait. Let's go for a walk.

> *They walk.* ESTHER *looks off into the distance and smiles.*

ESTHER: There you are. Finally.

> ESTHER *exits.*

MICHAEL: Strange, isn't it? How people continue walking down the street just like that, like nothing has changed. I'm walking down the same street I've been walking down my whole life and I'm thinking the buildings should be in a different order—

MUM: The trees in a different place.

MICHAEL: But it can't be. Can't change. Because this is where Dom is.

MUM: Here. Everywhere.

MICHAEL: Look, this whole place, it's like that music Dom used to play—too much bass so you end up dancing like your body parts don't fit together and laughing all at the same time. That's what this place is, the people who've been here bubbling up from the ground and spilling all over. It's girls in yellow underwear and hanging out in the McDonald's parking lot at night.

The Pontiac Trans Am appears.

It's that car and that car is Dom.

MUM: Unstoppable.

MICHAEL: I couldn't stop him. Couldn't change anything that night.

MUM: I know, but sometimes I can't stop thinking how much I want to be in that box.

They climb into the back seat of the car. DOM *in the driver's seat with one hand on the steering wheel and one arm out the window.*

MICHAEL: But you can't start the story over again. There's only moving forward. There's only lowered cars and people putting on their bests and strutting their stuff on Church Street—

MUM: And *Playboy* magazines and my best teapot buried under the front garden—

They pause and look at each other.

MICHAEL: And the boys who sag their pants and old houses being blown up and replaced with apartment buildings.

MUM *and* MICHAEL*'s faces are illuminated by a set of headlights, just as* DOM *and* MICHAEL*'s were towards the beginning of the play.* DOM *turns around and looks directly at* MUM. *She seems to see him for the first time. She holds out her hand tentatively and gently touches his cheek.*

SCENE EIGHT

The 'Fruit and Vegetables' sign flashes. LEENA *is leaving the fruit shop. Neither* MICHAEL *nor* MONIQUE *see her.* MICHAEL *is holding a stack of pancakes on a plate.* MONIQUE *is unpacking and arranging fruit.*

MONIQUE: You brought pancakes.

She reaches out to take them. MICHAEL *holds them back so that she can't reach them.*

MICHAEL: They're not for you.

MONIQUE: Oh.

MICHAEL: Why did you come to my apartment block that day and not come in?

MONIQUE: What?

MICHAEL: You came to my apartment building and sat outside with the mailboxes. Esther said you didn't come up because you weren't sure.

MONIQUE: I wasn't sure. Should I listen to my dad and not hang out with you or should I listen to you saying I should ignore my dad?

MICHAEL: What did you decide?

MONIQUE: I decided I'm not listening to either of you ... I was thinking about those girls throwing the tiles off the roof ... I get to decide what I want ...

> *There is the slamming of a door and they both jump a little before they turn around to see* MONIQUE'S DAD.

MONIQUE'S DAD: Again!

> MICHAEL *walks over and gives him the pancakes.* MONIQUE'S DAD *looks at* MICHAEL, *then the pancakes, and then at* MONIQUE.

My daughter says your brother died.

MICHAEL: Yes, sir.

MONIQUE'S DAD: No good. I lost my brother too. A long time ago. When I was young. Hard on mothers, but hard on brothers too.

> *He picks up a pancake and eats it slowly, looking at* MICHAEL.

[*Calling offstage to* JOE] Your sister's ... *special friend* is here. He wants to show you how to kick a ball without falling over.

MONIQUE: I get to decide what I want and ...

> *She gives* MICHAEL *a big kiss.* MONIQUE'S DAD *glares at them and aggressively eats the pancakes but does nothing.*

SCENE NINE

LEENA, POPPY, MUM *and* MICHAEL *sit in the living room of the apartment.* MUM *sees* DOM *and walks towards him. He gives her* The Fast and Furious *which she inserts into the DVD player. Scenes from the film begin to play on the screens.*

MICHAEL: [*to* LEENA] Why is Mum watching this?

LEENA: I think she's graduated.

POPPY: You know, out of the box.

LEENA: I think it's good. You know, first stop: Tokyo, Brazil or some island no-one's ever heard of.

POPPY: Next stop: outside her own apartment building.

MICHAEL: Church Street, Parramatta, the world!

MUM: I can hear you all, you know. I do know when you people are in the room with me. I do exist.

MICHAEL holds her hand.

MICHAEL: I haven't stopped knowing that you're real.

MUM: Even when I'm not really there?

A car crash scene plays silently in slow motion on the screens.

[*To* MICHAEL] There's no going back to the start of the story is there?

MICHAEL: No.

DOM: Whether I'm a quarter mile or a half a world away—

DOM smiles, puts his hands into his pockets and walks offstage. The rest of the family talk to each other and watch the DVD silently. The lights fade out on them but not on MICHAEL.

MICHAEL: [*to audience*] And that's how it happened. I saw him again in the hospital, the next day after the accident happened. And I knew it was Dom by the way he tilted his head slightly to the left and tucked his hands into the pockets of his saggy jeans. I could see he wasn't offering any kind of sadness … he was just saying goodbye.

He pulls out the notebook and begins to write. His words appear on the screen in giant handwritten letters: 'The Incredible Here and Now'.

THE END

RIVERSIDE | NATIONAL THEATRE OF PARRAMATTA

THE INCREDIBLE HERE AND NOW

13 — 22 July 2017

World Premiere at Riverside Theatres

Creative

Written and Adapted by	Felicity Castagna
Directors	Jeneffa Soldatic & Wayne Harrison
Set & Costume Designer	Isabel Hudson
Sound Designer	Séan Van Doornum
Lighting Designer	Martin Kinanne
Movement Director	Sara Black
Production Manager	Damion Holling
Stage Manager	Kirsty Walker
Creative Futures Participant	Concey Bosco
Drone Videographer	Tristan Baker

Cast

Michael	Bardiya McKinnon
Dom	Alex Cubis
Mum	Caroline Brazier
Shadi	Ryan Peters
Leena / Esther / Sal	Olivia Simone
Monique / Kate / Joe	Libby Asciak
Poppy / Principal / Monique's Dad	Sal Sharah

RIVERSIDE   PARRAMATTA VISIT · DISCOVER · EXPLORE AUSTRALIA'S NEXT GREAT CITY   NSW GOVERNMENT | Create NSW Arts, Screen & Culture   CROWN RESORTS FOUNDATION   PACKER FAMILY FOUNDATION

Playwright/Author's Note
Felicity Castagna

The Incredible Here and Now is a play about cars and boys and having to grow up too soon. The main character Michael knows everything about the community he lives in and through his stories, he lets the reader in; to the unsettled lives of his family members, the friends he meets in the McDonalds parking lot at night, the swimming pool where he meets the one girl who will acknowledge he's alive and the classmates who spend their mornings drooling at the Coke Factory on their walk to school. Parramatta is one of the play's main characters and through a close look at the small and intimate places it is made up of, the text explores the ways in which the places where we are shape who we are right now and what we might become.

Fundamentally it is also a play about language and silence. Our personal grief is such a fundamentally hard thing to articulate, whether you're a teenage boy or a mother. That grief therefore needed to be expressed in the visual language of the play; a box, a stack of pancakes, an older brother who is not there anymore but continually returns to stage like a memory that is always in the back of one's mind.

The original book the play is based on was written in vignettes, a kind of short-short story with heightened poetic imagery. It is meant to be like taking a picture of a moment in time and committing it to words. I have tried to capture this in the writing of the play. The sense that life is made up of these small moments of time that we think of as ordinary but are really quite extraordinary if we examine them a little closer. That is what Michael does, after all; he is a writer.

I would like to thank the National Theatre of Parramatta, particularly Robert Love and Joanne Kee for their faith in me, and Wayne Harrison and Jeneffa Soldatic for their direction and mentoring. I would also like to thank the actors involved in both the play and the script development week for their generous and thoughtful feedback on my script.

Director's Notes
Jeneffa Soldatic

'Nothing bad could
ever happen here.'

Growing up in the Western Suburbs
was never dull or conventional, rather
it was always exciting and loud. We
are a multi-ethnic community who,
together, are a family. Our front
door was constantly opened to the
sound of a neighbour screaming into
the house, 'Hello Mrs Sol', followed
by 'putting the kettle on'. No-one
ever felt out of place in each other's
homes as our unspoken rule was,
all are welcomed. My sister even
married the boy across the street,
that's just how close the community
can get.

My youth, like our characters, was
filled with cars, boys, going to the
pool, and the unfortunate accidents
that interminably crashed on our
corner. My childhood road is freshly
decorated with the recently added
crosses and old eternal shrines
for our beloved local boys who
dangerously had too much fun and
drove themselves too fast to meet
their fate.

When I first moved out of the West,
I befriended every neighbour in my
apartment building. I assumed that
everyone in Bondi knew all their
seven neighbours and that they
would pop on over for a cuppa tea
to share their stories of the day. My
door was always open but rarely
frequented and even in New York my
kettle was only occasionally used by
my friendly neighbours.

There is a kinship and an
understanding with us Westies, an
ownership of our stories that are an
important part of the tapestry of our
local community, and a need for our
voice to be heard. Felicity Castagna
has given us one of the local stories
in *The Incredible Here and Now* and
the National Theatre of Parramatta a
place for that story to be heard.

Bardiya McKinnon | Michael

25-year-old Bardiya McKinnon started acting at the age of 14 where he saw his first role in the SBS police drama *East West 101*. He got his first major role at the age of 15 on the Disney Channel's *As the Bell Rings*, which he starred in for four years. In 2013 he starred in the Channel 7 teen drama *In Your Dreams*, the filming of which took place across Sydney and Germany. During the course of filming he was able to write original music for the TV show and hopes to further his career not only as an actor but as a producer and singer/songwriter. Credits in the theatre include the role of Georg in the successful 2016 run of the hit musical *Spring Awakening* by ATYP. Bardiya also appeared as Clive in the Australian premiere of Stuart Slade's West End success *BU21*. Bardiya is currently producing his first show, *DNA* by Dennis Kelly for Sydney Fringe, a show he will also star in.

Libby Asciak | Monique / Kate / Joe

Hailing from Melbourne, Libby moved to Sydney to study at NIDA. She received the Robertson Family Trust scholarship and graduated with a Diploma in Music Theatre. After graduating she moved to Perth to study at the Western Australian Academy of Performing Arts (WAAPA), graduating with a Bachelor in Music Theatre. Since graduating Libby has continued working on her craft with acclaimed teachers such as Larry Moss, Colette Mann and Les Chantery. In 2015 Libby originated the role of Heather Duke in the Australian premiere of *Heathers The Musical* (Showwork/Hayes Theatre Co/QPAC). Libby's TV credits include: *Neighbours* (Fremantle Media), *Here Come the Habibs!* and most recently the role of Rachel Rossi in *The Secret Daughter* (Screentime).

Caroline Brazier | Mum

Caroline Brazier is a NIDA graduate, perhaps best known for her ongoing role as Wendy, the long-suffering ex-wife of Cleaver Greene, in the ABC's *Rake*.

Caroline has worked extensively in theatre, television and film, including for Bell Shakespeare, Queensland Theatre Company, Melbourne Theatre Company, Black Swan, Sydney Theatre Company, La Mama, Belvoir, Rock Surfers, and Griffin Theatre Company. She will be playing the lead role in Moira Buffini's *Dinner* for the Sydney Theatre Company in 2017.

Caroline played Chrissy in the first two seasons of *Packed to the Rafters*, and has enjoyed roles on *Wild Boys* and *Home and Away*, amongst many others, and is soon appearing in *Offspring*.

Caroline also stars in the new Australian feature film *Pulse*, which premiered at the 2017 Sydney Film Festival. She won the Sydney Theatre Critics' award for her work in Toby Schmitz' play *I Want to Sleep with Tom Stoppard*, and had been nominated for an AACTA for her work in *Rake*.

Alex Cubis | Dom

After working on various independent films and shorts in Sydney, Alex appeared in a lead role in 26 episodes of *Mako Mermaids*, a Netflix original series. In between seasons, Alex performed on stage in many venues including the New Theatre and Parade Playhouse. He also filmed a role on the most recent season of the award-winning ABC series *Rake*, and prior to that appeared in a major role in the successful online series *The Gauntlet*, released on Amazon and SparkkTV. *Show Offs* and *No Evil*, film projects in which he appeared in lead roles, were selected for numerous festivals including the Oscar-qualifying Palm Springs International Short Fest 2016, Cleveland International Film Festival and 2017 Internationale Kurzfilmwoche Regensburg in Germany.

Alex recently wrapped a lead role on feature film *Just Within Reach*, starring Estella Warren (*Planet of The Apes*), the YouTube pilot *Nia* and the mockumentary online comedy series *Unverified*, all shot in Los Angeles. He also currently hosts a weekly podcast for iTunes about artistic perspectives, *Honest Conversations with Alex Cubis*. He is a graduate of the University of Sydney, where he studied Bachelor of Arts/Bachelor of Laws, and is currently an academic lecturer at the same institution.

Ryan Peters | Shadi

Ryan Peters graduated from ACTT, renamed AFTT, with an Advanced Diploma of Stage and Screen Acting. Currently he's with Suzie Steen Management and has performed in a series of plays, such as AFTT's *Coriolanus* (where he played Coriolanus) and *The Last Days of Judas Iscariot* (where he played Sigmund Freud and Butch Honeywell) both performed at Belvoir. He played the role of Evan in Darlo Drama's production of *Don's Party*, directed by Sean O'Riordan and performed at The New Theatre. From 2009 until the present, he has performed and taught with an acting troupe called ACTiv Elite Performers, where he's performed in a number of productions both self-devised and professionally written. Ryan has always believed that all art is allegorical and autobiographical in some way and he's always loved acting and telling stories to people.

Sal Sharah | Poppy / Principal / Monique's Dad

Sal was most recently seen in *Hakawati* for National Theatre of Parramatta/Sydney Festival. Other theatre credits include *Jump for Jordan* (Griffin Theatre Company); *Miss Julie*, *The Rise and Fall of Little Voice* (Sydney Theatre Company); *Les Enfants du Paradis* (Belvoir); *Felliniada* (Belvoir/Auto de Fe); *Salome* (Crossroads); *My Son the Lawyer is Drowning* (Ensemble Theatre); *Alex & Eve* (Bulldog Theatre Company); His musical theatre highlights include the original Australian productions of *Grease*, *Godspell*, *The Rocky Horror Show* and Reg Livermore's *Ned Kelly* as well as roles in *My Fair Lady*, *Sunset Boulevard*, *Guys and Dolls*, *Great Expectations* and *The Gambler*. Television includes *The Code*, *Rake*, *East West 101*, *All Saints*, *Wild Side*, *GP*, *Heartbreak High* and *Restless Years*. Films include *Alex & Eve*, *The Boys*, *Chain Reaction*, *Hostage* and *The Custodian*.

Olivia Simone | Leena / Esther / Sal

Olivia is a writer, actress and producer currently living and working in LA and Australia. She trained at NIDA and since graduating has worked professionally for the past 10 years. Her TV and film appearances include All Saints, Love My Way, Winners and Losers, Dance Academy, Hobby Farm and has toured Nationally with Bell Shakespeare Company, playing Ophelia, Juliet and Lady Macbeth.

She played Viola for Night Sky Production's 12th Knight. Hermia for the Australian Shakespeare Company, Virginia in The Australian Theatre Company playing Virginia US premiere of Ruben Guthrie in Los Angeles, Loretta in The Girl Who Loved The Beatles for her own company; performing in Sydney and LA nominated for best international play. Olivia is the founding director of Off THE BEATEN TRACK PRODUCTIONS (OTBTP) and has also written and will star in the feature film Running on Perfect Time an Italian and Australian co production.

Felicity Castagna | Playwright & Author

Felicity Castagna is the author of the multi award-winning novel, *The Incredible Here and Now* and its stage adaptation. Her collection of short stories, *Small Indiscretions,* was named an ABR book of the year. Her work has appeared on ABC Radio and TV as well as in many national journals and newspapers. Her latest novel is *No More Boats.* She holds a PhD from Western Sydney University and teaches creative writing all over Australia. She hosts the storytelling night, Studio Stories, at the Parramatta Artists Studios and is the Director of Finishing School, a mentorship program for women writers in western Sydney.

Jeneffa Soldatic | Director

Jeneffa Soldatic is from Ingleburn NSW. She received her MFA from the Actors Studio Drama School in New York City, and is a proud life member of the Actors Studio. She performed in *Al Takes a Bride* (Actors Studio), *The Guardian Angel* (Living Theatre, by personal invitation from Judith Malina), *Curb Your Enthusiasm, The Tonight Show with Jay Leno* and toured singing with The Polyphonic Spree, supporting David Bowie. A member of the Actors Studio Directors Unit, she has directed and developed numerous award winning theatre and film productions internationally, including *Be Careful What You Wish For* (Edinburgh Fringe Festival), *Dolores*, and *The Girl Who Loved the Beatles.* She recently directed *Mrs President* and the series *Then That Happened in NYC* and also the award-winning production of *Speaking in Tongues* for Australian Theatre Company in Los Angeles. Jeneffa is an on-set acting coach to many accomplished international actors and also at major international drama schools. She is grateful as a proud acting member of the Actors Studio to be invited to the new Directors Unit of the Actors Studio in NYC under multi-award-winner Estelle Parsons. Jeneffa would like to thank Wayne Harrison for inviting her to share the directing role, bringing her back to her home in the Western Suburbs. This is Jeneffa's first production with National Theatre of Parramatta.

Wayne Harrison | Director

Wayne Harrison AM, is the former Director/CEO of Sydney Theatre Company where he directed over 50 productions, including the award-winning *Into the Woods*, *Six Degrees of Separation*, *Shadowlands*, *Two Weeks with the Queen* and David Williamson's *Dead White Males*. For Spiegelworld International, productions he has written and directed include: *Absinthe, Desir, Empire* (all in New York), *Vegas Nocturne* (Las Vegas) and Absinthe (Miami and Las Vegas). His production of *Absinthe* at Caesar's Palace in Las Vegas is now in its seventh year. Recent credits include *Hakawati* (National Theatre of Parramatta/Sydney Festiva), *Nest Half Empty* (Arts Club Theatre, Vancouver), Louis Nowra's *Cosi* (Kingshead Theatre, London) and Human Nature's *Jukebox* (Australian stadium tour & PBS television special, Las Vegas). His first production at Riverside was *Othello* in 1988; subsequent productions have included Don Reid's *Codgers*, Annie Byron's *RU4Me* and Justin Fleming's *Shellshock*. He is a member of the Directorate of the National Theatre of Parramatta.

This is Wayne's second production with National Theatre of Parramatta.

Isabel Hudson | Set & Costume Designer

Isabel is a Sydney-based production designer and graduate of the NIDA design course (2015). She holds a Bachelor of Arts (Screen and Sound) from the University of New South Wales (2012). Isabel was awarded the William Fletcher Foundation Tertiary Grant for emerging artists in 2015. Recently, Isabel has designed set and costumes for *Intersection* (ATYP), *The Shadowbox, Hurt* (White Box Productions), *The Block Universe, Journey's End* (Cross Pollinate), *The Chamber Pot Opera* (Bontom; Sydney, Adelaide and Edinburgh seasons), *Slut* (Festival Fatale), *Blackrock* (White Box at the Seymour Centre) and worked as an associate on Opera Australia's *My Fair Lady*. In 2015 Isabel designed for Strindberg's *A Dream Play* (directed by Kim Carpenter), *Top Girls* (directed by Susanna Dowling), *Love and Honour and Pride and Pity and Compassion and Sacrifice* (directed by Priscilla Jackman).

Isabel's upcoming productions include *One Flew over the Cuckoo's Nest* (Sport for Jove), *I Love You Now* (Darlinghurst Theatre Co.), *The Plant* (Ensemble Theatre Company) and *The Merry Widow* (Opera Australia – Assistant Set Designer to Michael Scott Mitchell). Isabel tutors in design communication for the design program at NIDA. This is Isabel's first production with National Theatre of Parramatta.

Séan Van Doornum | Sound Designer

Seán graduated from the Sydney Conservatorium of Music with a Bachelor of Composition. Seán has been the recipient of several awards including the Allan Zavod Jazz/Classical Composition Award and the ArtStart Grant from the Australia Council, and was a finalist in the 2011 APRA Professional Development Award.

In 2011 Seán composed the original score for the Australian premiere of *The Libertine* (Stephen Jefrey) by Sport For Jove Theatre Company. Seán then moved to New York where he worked at Atlantic Sound Studios, and also composed for several theatre productions such as *Alice In Teresa's Land* (Lupe Gehrenbeck), which premiered at The Producer's Club. During this time Sean was fortunate enough to work, record and perform with musicians such as Shahzad Ismaily (Elvis Costello, Yoko Ono, Laurie Anderson), Michael League (Snarky Puppy) and Ches Smith (Marc Ribot, John Zorn), and also performed with his band eüsh at renowned NYC venues such as Joe's Pub, Pianos, Bowery Electric, Rockwood Music Hall and Spike Hill.

In 2015 Seán composed for an IMAX feature film *The Earth Wins*. In 2016 he worked as Music Supervisor for the Australian Theatre Company's award winning production of *Speaking In Tongues* (Andrew Bovell) at The Matrix Theatre in Hollywood, California.

This is Seán's first production with National Theatre of Parramatta.

Martin Kinanne | Lighting Designer

Martin has designed for theatre and events both nationally and internationally. He has lit shows for Ensemble Theatre (*Six Dance Lessons in Six Weeks, End of the Rainbow* and *Kids Stuff*); Sydney Opera House (*Love Loss and What I Wore* and *Celebrity Autobiography*); Bell Shakespeare (*R&J, Just Macbeth*); Darlinghurst Theatre Company (*I Love You Now*); White Box Theatre (*The Hatpin, Love Song, LoveBITES, Bang, Belongings, Unholy Ghosts* and *Blackrock*); Monkey Baa (*Fairy's Wings, Worry Worts, Bugalugs Bum Thief* and *Sprung*); Doorstop Arts (*Next To Normal, Dogfight*); Griffin Theatre Company (*Satango, The House On The Lake*); The Production Company (*Sunset Boulevard* and *Promises, Promises*); and CheepUk in the Theatre Nesle, Paris (*Letter To Larry*).

Work beyond the theatrical includes the Hamer Hall Opening Celebrations in 2012; East Timor's Independence Day Celebrations for the United Nations; *Absinthe, Desir* and *Empire* for Spiegelworld (New York, Las Vegas, Miami, Australia, New Zealand, Canada and Japan); the Papal Ceremonies at World Youth Day 2008; and White Night in Melbourne 2017. Martin is possibly best known for his spectacularly theatrical lighting of the Sydney Harbour Bridge (the Bridge Effect) from 2000 to 2007 for New Year's Eve, which has brought him international renown.

This is Martin's second production with National Theatre of Parramatta.

Sara Black | Movement Director

With a Bachelor of Dance from the Victorian College of the Arts, Sara has worked as a choreographer, performer, teacher and collaborator in Australia and internationally over the past 12 years. Her choreographic credits include *Jasper Jones, Seventeen, Peter Pan* (Belvoir); *Girls Like That* (ATYP); *#Killallmen* (NIDA); *Taction* (Sydney Dance Company); *Act Of Contact* (QL2); *E-volve* (CDDC); *Pitch Black* (Seekae); *Sensation, Trigger, Action* (Flipside); *Fresh Produce* (Rogue, Next Wave Festival); *Gravitas* (short film, currently in development). Her assistant choreographic credits include *Obsidian* (Iceland Dance Company); *Shane Warne the Musical* (Eddy Perfect and Neil Armfield); and *Woyzeck* (Malthouse Theatre). Sara's short works include *Value for Money* (London premiere); *InAnimate* (Lucy Guerin Inc); *Parental Guidance Recommended* (Dancehouse) and *TunnelVisioned* (Short Film Dancehouse). As a founding member of Rogue dance collective, Sara co-created and choreographed new works *Puck, Ocular Proof* and *Persona*. Over the last eleven years she has performed and collaborated with Punchdrunk (UK), Protein Dance (UK), The Australian Ballet, Lucy Guerin Inc, NYID (David Pledger) and as a main collaborator and performer for Gideon Obarzanek's Chunky Move where she toured extensively internationally. In 2008 she was awarded a Helpmann Award for best performer in a dance/physical theatre piece and has since been nominated for two Green Room awards in the same category. Sara has worked extensively with both Australian and international independent artists including Narelle Benjamin, Erna Omarsdottir, Damien Jalet, Martin Del Amo, Elissa Goodrich, Bagryana Popov, Stephanie Lake, Lloyd Newson, Wendy Houstoun, Carlee Mellow, Antony Hamilton and Byron Perry.

This is Sara's first production with National Theatre of Parramatta.

Damion Holling | Production Manager

Damion is a highly experienced site and production manager with experience across theatre and events. He has been the Site Construction Manager for over seven years at Sydney Festival and is also the resident Production Manager for multiple Sydney based theatre companies. His work showcases locally, nationally and internationally. Damion has a long history with National Theatre of Parramatta and is thrilled to carry on his involvement with them on the next exciting project.

This is Damion's fourth production with National Theatre of Parramatta.

Kirsty Walker | Stage Manager

This is Kirsty's third production with the National Theatre of Parramatta, having previously worked on *The Cartographer's Curse* and *Smurf in Wanderland*. Her credits as Stage Manager also include: for Don't Look Away: *Inner Voices, The Legend of King O'Malley* (for which she was also FOH Mixer); for the Glynn Nicholas Group: *Song Contest: The Almost Eurovision Experience*. Kirsty's credits as Assistant Stage Manager include: for Belvoir St Theatre: *Kill the Messenger*; for Melbourne Opera: *The Abduction from the Seraglio, Anna Bolena, Tannhäuser*. She was the FOH Mixer in the 2015 Edinburgh Festival Fringe. Kirsty is a NIDA (Production) graduate.

Concey Bosco | Creative Futures Participant

Concey Bosco is a graduate from Excelsia College (formerly Wesley Institute), with a Bachelor of Dramatic Art. Her production highlights include: lighting design for *Much Ado About Nothing* (Excelsia College); and stage management for *Sweet Charity* (Hayes Theatre Co), *Who Speaks For Me* (National Theatre of Parramatta), *Superhal The Puzzle, Simpson J, 202, Away* (Liverpool Performing Arts Ensemble), *Interior, Miss Reardon Drinks A Little* (Excelsia College), *Hairspary Jr, Fame Jr* (South Eastern Musicals), and *A Murder Is Announced* (Genesian Theatre). She directed *Interior* and *Crossfire* (Excelsia College).

Performance highlights include: *Act Three, Scene Five, Faust, A Thousand Cranes, The Main Thing* and *Blood Wedding* (Excelsia College) and *The Outsiders* (CPAC YOUTH). Concey loves the theatre and enjoys every aspect of a theatrical production and is pursuing directing in the near future.

Creative Futures Program

The Creative Futures Program provides on-the-job learning and networking opportunities for creatives, production and backstage people, with the scheme enabling each participant to advance their careers within their nominated field.

National Theatre of Parramatta
Riverside's Resident Company

Having burst onto the Australian theatre scene in 2016 with four acclaimed new theatre productions, National Theatre of Parramatta (NTofP) continues in 2017 with four world premieres, exciting commissions and creative developments which we look forward to sharing with you in the future.

NTofP aspires to create bold, contemporary works that draw their inspiration from the rich diversity of Western Sydney and beyond, adding to our cultural landscape is a company that reflects the nation on stage.

Integral to our Company is the development of Western Sydney's professional and emerging artists.

We aim to build generations of exciting and challenging theatre-makers, capable of making work of the highest quality for a range of audiences, with and for National Theatre of Parramatta and the wider theatre sector.

In 2016, NTofP launched a range of behind the scenes programs that build capacity for the performing arts in New South Wales with playwriting, mentorships, professional and creative development, industry talks, networking opportunities, engagement for young people and audience outreach.

Support Us

We believe in developing work that celebrates the richness of our society, and its creative talent, and in the importance of providing opportunities for artists, writers and directors to develop their skills.

Whether you are an individual wishing to become a patron or make a donation, or a company seeking partnership opportunities, your support is invaluable to our continuing efforts to deliver exceptional work to the widest possible audience.

Every donation is valuable. All donations of $2 or more are tax-deductible. Donations can be made through Parramatta Cultural Trust.

For more information visit our website or contact Executive Producer, Joanne Kee.

02 8839 3385
jkee@nationaltheatreofparramatta.com.au

RIVERSIDE   PARRAMATTA
VISIT · DISCOVER · EXPLORE
AUSTRALIA'S NEXT GREAT CITY   NSW GOVERNMENT | Create NSW Arts, Screen & Culture   CROWN RESORTS FOUNDATION   PACKER FAMILY FOUNDATION

Staff & Thank Yous

National Theatre of Parramatta

Directorate	Annette Shun Wah
	S. Shakthidharan
	Wayne Harrison AM
Executive Producer	Joanne Kee
Company Coordinator	Clare Spillman
Marketing Coordinator	Claire Cornu
Administrator	Cassandra Bayley
Traineeship	Stephanie Dellzeit

Riverside Theatres

Director	Robert Love AM
Business Manager	Pamela Thornton
Operations Manager	Linda Taylor
Marketing & Comms Manager	Jonathan Llewellyn

PR & Media

Kabuku PR

Thank You

Nicholas Brown
Andrea Demetriades
Olivia Rose
Bali Padda
Fiona Press
William Zappa
Gary Hunter
Patrick Nalletamby
The Pontiac Car Club of Australia
Pic n Payless
Ivor Indyk, Giramondo
Tristan Baker, BAM Studios
Peter Beaumont & The Sydney Dragway
Jim Campbell

National Theatre of Parramatta

Corner of Church & Market Streets
Parramatta NSW 2151

+61 2 8839 3385
admin@nationaltheatreofparramatta.com.au
nationaltheatreofparramatta.com.au

f National Theatre of Parramatta
@ntofp
@NTofP

#ntofp #ntofpincredible

www.currency.com.au

Visit Currency Press' website now to:

- Order books
- Browse through our full list of titles including plays, screenplays, theory and criticism, performance handbooks, educational texts and more
- Choose a play for your school or performance group by cast specs
- Seek performance rights
- Find out about performing arts news
- For students: read our study guides
- For teachers: access free curriculum information and teacher notes

We are also on Facebook and Instagram (@currencypress). Join the conversation!

The performing arts publisher